IMAGES OF WAR

NAZI CONCENTRATION CAMP COMMANDANTS 1933-1945

RARE PHOTOGRAPHS FROM WARTIME ARCHIVES

Ian Baxter

D1567368

Pen & Sword
MILITARY

First published in Great Britain in 2014 by
PEN & SWORD MILITARY
An imprint of
Pen & Sword Books Ltd
47 Church Street
Barnsley
South Yorkshire
S70 2AS

Copyright © Ian Baxter, 2014

ISBN 978-1-78159-388-2

The right of Ian Baxter to be identified as author of this work has been asserted by him in accordance with the Copyright, Designs and Patents Act 1988.

A CIP catalogue record for this book is available from the British Library.

All rights reserved. No part of this book may be reproduced or transmitted in any form or by any means, electronic or mechanical including photocopying, recording or by any information storage and retrieval system, without permission from the Publisher in writing.

Typeset by Concept, Huddersfield, West Yorkshire HD4 5JL.
Printed and bound in England by Page Bros, Norwich.

Pen & Sword Books Ltd incorporates the imprints of Pen & Sword Archaeology, Atlas, Aviation, Battleground, Discovery, Family History, History, Maritime, Military, Naval, Politics, Railways, Select, Social History, Transport, True Crime, and Claymore Press, Frontline Books, Leo Cooper, Praetorian Press, Remember When, Seaforth Publishing and Wharncliffe.

For a complete list of Pen & Sword titles please contact
PEN & SWORD BOOKS LIMITED
47 Church Street, Barnsley, South Yorkshire, S70 2AS, England
E-mail: enquiries@pen-and-sword.co.uk
Website: www.pen-and-sword.co.uk

Contents

About the Author

Ian Baxter is a military historian who specialises in German twentieth-century military history. He has written more than forty books including *Poland – The Eighteen Day Victory March, Panzers in North Africa, The Ardennes Offensive, The Western Campaign, The 12th SS Panzer-Division Hitlerjugend, The Waffen-SS on the Western Front, The Waffen-SS on the Eastern Front, The Red Army at Stalingrad, Elite German Forces of World War II, Armoured Warfare, German Tanks of War, Blitzkrieg, Panzer-Divisions at War, Hitler's Panzers, German Armoured Vehicles of World War Two, Last Two Years of the Waffen-SS at War, German Soldier Uniforms and Insignia, German Guns of the Third Reich, Defeat to Retreat: The Last Years of the German Army at War 1943–1945, Operation Bagration – the destruction of Army Group Centre, German Guns of the Third Reich, Rommel and the Afrika Korps, U-Boat War,* and most recently *The Sixth Army, the Road to Stalingrad, German Mountain Troops,* and *Himmler's Nazi Concentration Camp Guards.* He has also written over 100 articles including 'Last Days of Hitler', 'Wolf's Lair', 'Story of the V1 and V2 Rocket Programme', 'Secret Aircraft of World War Two', 'Rommel At Tobruk', 'Hitler's War with his Generals', 'Secret British Plans to Assassinate Hitler', 'SS At Arnhem', 'Hitlerjugend', 'Battle Of Caen 1944', 'Gebirgsjäger at War', 'Panzer Crews', 'Hitlerjugend Guerrillas', 'Last Battles in the East', 'Battle of Berlin' and many more. He has also reviewed numerous military studies for publication, supplied thousands of photographs and important documents to various publishers and film production companies worldwide, and lectures to various schools, colleges and universities throughout the United Kingdom and Southern Ireland.

Introduction

Concentration Camp Commandants is a reassessment of the men who were in charge of many of the largest work and mass murder camps in Europe, where they often ordered the killing of tens of thousands of people. Drawing on published and unpublished material and the handwritten memoirs of some of these commandants, the book is a compelling and chilling story told through the eyes of these terrible men, and those who knew them. The book describes vividly daily life at these camps and reveals diaries from staff and friends, describing in detail their brutal hold over the camps both against their own staff and those interned. This book reassesses their psychological personalities and produces evidence that sometimes these men were not all sadistic unhinged brutes like many other concentration camp commanders. Yet many of them were mass murderers. Most of the commandants were eager to please, and keen to show their superiors they were great innovators in the way they organised the killing process. They often undertook their mammoth tasks of extermination like competent businessman. For instance, Rudolf Höss had, within just three years of becoming commandant of Auschwitz, turned the previously quiet and secluded complex there into the largest mass murder factory in the history of the world. But behind this barbarism Höss was a husband and father. On the edge of the Auschwitz main camp Frau Höss and her well-groomed children lived 'in more or less harmony'. Here she baked cakes, cooked German homemade dishes, ensured the gardens were tended lovingly and the wine cellar was well stocked. Each day Rudolf would arrive home following a hard day masterminding the killing of thousands. And yet he clearly struggled with his task. Often he would take himself off at night and stand out at the gas chambers or at the burnings, and was forced to think of his wife and children without connecting them to the horrors that were taking place nearby. But in spite of the constant pressures Höss, like so many other commandants, remained throughout fixated to the last on command and obedience. The commandants believed whole-heartedly that no one else could perform as well as they could in such terrible circumstances. In the end, whilst waiting sentence for their crimes, no shock could disturb their conviction that in their eyes they had always done right and that they had done their duty conscientiously, attentively, and to everyone's satisfaction.

The story of Concentration Camp Commandants from early beginnings to the mass murder of millions of innocent souls is a gripping narration and a valuable addition to Holocaust studies. It is a disturbing portrayal of some of the most notorious men in the Nazi regime and an incredible insight into the mind of mass murderers.

Concentration Camps

The first concentration camps were erected in Germany in February 1933. Primarily these camps were used to house and torture political opponents and union organisers. The camps held some 45,000 prisoners and during the mid- to late-1930s these camps were greatly expanded. When *SS-Reichsführer* Heinrich Himmler took control of the concentration camp system throughout Germany he started using the camps' facilities and personnel to purge German society of so-called racially undesirable elements such as Jews, criminals, homosexuals, Jehovah's witnesses, Gypsies and any other elements deemed a threat to Nazi rule. The concentration camps were administered by the Concentration Camps Inspectorate which in 1942 was merged into *SS-Wirtschafts-Verwaltungshauptamt* and were guarded by *SS-Totenkopfverbände*.

As early as1940 the situation in the concentration camps had become untenable due to the new policies of arresting and detaining enemies of the State. News had already circulated through SS channels that government officials were now demanding immediate action in the expansion of the concentration camp system throughout Germany and its new conquered territory, Poland. The German authorities quickly pressed forward to establish various camps where the arrested could be incarcerated and set to work as stonebreakers and construction workers for buildings and streets. It was envisaged that these people would remain as a slave labour force, and it was therefore deemed necessary to erect these so called 'quarantine camps' in order to subdue the local population. Initially, it had been proposed that the 'quarantine camps' were to hold the prisoners until they were sent to the various other concentration camps in the *Reich*. However, it soon became apparent that this purpose was totally impracticable. So it was approved that these camps were to function as a permanent prison for all those who were unfortunate enough to have been sent there.

The thousands of concentration camps that were built across Europe functioned as a whole very well, albeit run barbarically by the individual camp commandants. Under their strict command a number of the camps were constructed by the inmates themselves. Every day the prisoners were forced to work in all weather conditions often without a break and continuously being subjected to appalling brutality. Despite the conditions the commandants were determined to get the prisoners to complete the buildings no matter how it was done. Most of the buildings that were built served merely to house and provide the basic needs of the prisoners, guards and SS staff that ran the camp.

Once the camps were built some of them were used not just to incarcerate the prisoners, but to force them to work as slave labour. This consisted of making them work either inside the camp itself, or in moving them to various sub-camps where the prisoners would work in factories, often for large German-owned companies. This was very lucrative for the SS and the companies that became involved.

As the concentration camp system grew and new polices evolved some of the camps became dual purpose: labour and death camps. Other camps too were constructed as death camps: their only function was to murder. In direct response to the growing demand in concentration camps the SS needed civilian expertise to help install heating systems, electrical gear, and sewage systems, and also to build chimneys, and other buildings such as crematoria. Many civilian companies were involved, in their professional capacity, with genocide, with lots of them eager to produce the goods for the SS for financial reward.

Chapter One

Camp Indoctrination

Many SS men who entered the realms of the concentration camp system welcomed the chance of joining this elite organisation because of its strict system of beliefs and values based on the military virtues of obedience and self-discipline. They sought the idea of becoming part of the SS not purely because it was the racial-ideological elite, but for status reasons and the chance to become part of an organisation that could possibly control the course of Germany's path to recovery. Joining the SS also meant camaraderie and career prospects.

Reichsführer Heinrich Himmler, commander of the SS, had made considerable efforts to recruit members of the old German elite and, through a tactful combination of pressure and adulation, to invite many fighters of the old 'German Guard' to give up their daily jobs and become full-time members of what became known as the black order of the new '*SS Staat*'. Within months many of these new recruits had formally joined the SS, and were soon assigned to run the various new concentration camps that had sprung up across Germany.

One of the earliest camps, called Dachau, would be regarded as the foundation of all other camps. *SS-Brigadeführer* Theodor Eicke had been made commander of Dachau concentration camp in June 1933, and became a major figure in the SS. He was regarded as the architect, builder, and director of the concentration camp system and ruled it with an iron fist. As a man he was stocky in appearance, blatantly brutal and ruthless, and gave off an aura of raw energy.

Dachau was located on the grounds of an abandoned munitions factory near the medieval town of Dachau, ten miles northwest of Munich. It was the first regular concentration camp established by the National Socialist government and was regarded by Himmler as the first camp for political opponents who were seen as an imminent threat to the new German government. Dachau was established on 20 March 1933, and it served as a prototype and model for the other concentration camps that followed. Its basic organisation, camp layout, and construction of buildings were developed and ordered by Theodor Eicke.

Dachau was not like a normal prison. Here, the inmates did not know how long their sentences would run. They led an existence of uncertainty when they would see freedom again. Life for the prisoners inside Dachau was brutal. The SS guards were all ordered to follow Eicke's demand for blind and absolute obedience and to treat each prisoner with fanatical hatred. By perpetually drilling his SS guards to hate the prisoners, they were able to infuse themselves with anger and mete out severe punishments. The training which the SS guards were given at the camp was relentless. They learned about enemies of the state, and were given an in-depth indoctrination into SS philosophy and racial superiority. These ideological teachings were aimed at producing men who ardently believed in the new Aryan order. Regularly the SS staff had to listen to the commandant lecturing them about anti-Semitism. On the notice boards inside the SS barracks and canteen there were copies of the racist newspaper 'Der Stürmer'. Propaganda newspapers were deliberately pinned up in order to foment hatred and violence against the prisoners, and to encourage anti-Semitic behaviour among the staff, especially the younger men. In Eicke's view, once his staff had learnt their trade of brutality without the slightest compunction, the commandant had absolute power over them.

All of the staff at Dachau were indoctrinated into a fanatical determination to serve the SS with blind allegiance. Eicke invested each SS man with life-and-death power over all the inmates of the camp. Rule breaking among the prisoners was classified as a crime. It was looked upon as an incitement to disobedience and each guard was given power to handout stringent punishments.

The Dachau formula for mistreating the inmates sometimes affected the guards, but as members of the SS they were compelled to implement orders to be cruel to the prisoners with horrific efficiency. All SS were given extensive freedom to deal very harshly with any inmates they deemed to have committed a crime 'behind the wire'. In addition to the general physical abuse meted out to the prisoners the camp commandant introduced other measures of cruelty upon these hapless individuals. Prisoners were deprived of warm food for up to four days, they were subjected to long periods of solitary confinement on a diet of bread and water. To supplement these harsh methods Eicke introduced corporal punishment into the daily routine. A prisoner would receive twenty-five strokes with the lash, carried out in the open square on specific orders of the commandant in the presence of assembled SS guards. In order to ensure every SS officer, non-commissioned officer and SS guard was infused with the same brutal mentality as their commandant, Eicke regularly ensured that each man routinely punished prisoners with the lash without showing the slightest hesitancy, emotion or, most of all, remorse. Only in this way could Eicke guarantee that his concentration camp staff would become hardened to the brutal code that he himself had harshly implemented.

Eicke also infused his staff with hatred against Jews, emigrants, homosexuals and Jehovah Witnesses. Frequently the SS men listened whilst the commandant brazenly delivered lectures about what he considered were the most dangerous enemies of National Socialism.

Predominantly, he instructed his men to be brutal to the Jews and use whatever violence necessary to keep them in check. However, often the Jews were only seen at roll calls. For long periods, sometimes up to four months, they were shut away in sealed barracks only ever being allowed to leave their beds at mealtimes and roll call.

Although some of the staff disliked the brutality of the camp, most were none-theless inspired by its harsh order and discipline. They were able to bury their emotions and become absorbed by loyalty to the SS. Some would hope that in the future they might run their own concentration camp. In spite of the crude and brutal values of the SS, it offered many of these men a clear example to follow. They saw Dachau as a stepping-stone to success within the realms of the SS order.

Regular beatings and cruel acts of brutality continued to escalate at Dachau. Most SS men became pitiless and callously thoughtless to human suffering, and their thirst for moving through the ranks far outweighed any moral feelings. They became increasingly convinced that the camp was the most effective instrument available for destroying all elements hostile to the banner of National Socialism.

Most of the SS were motivated by Eicke's success and his firm grip on his own position within the camp. They watched how the commandant strengthened his power in order to make the camp run more efficiently. They saw the camp evolve and watched Eicke organise Dachau into a model detention centre with its various administration departments. There was a medical department, an administration pay office to purchase all supplies, another office to retain all the personal property sur-rendered by the inmates upon entering the camp, a department for repair and maintenance, and one for the making of the prisoner's uniforms.

Eicke's staff also observed how he had organized the inmates to work and expand the camp's economic enterprises. They saw how the commandant put to work the prisoners to construct buildings, and to expand the camp to include a locksmith's shop, a saddlery, and a shoemaking and table shop.

Eicke was a great believer that the inmates were able to endure prison with more discipline if they were allowed to work. For him working in slavery was a mystical declaration that self-sacrifice through endless labour would bring about a kind of spiritual freedom. It was this belief that prompted Eicke to display the inscription 'Arbeit Macht Frei' ('Work Brings Freedom') on the main entrance gate of Dachau. The slogan itself was not new to the National Socialists.

For some of Eicke's staff their post to Dachau was to mould their future in the ranks of the SS. Not only would it offer them officer status and a regular wage for them and their families, but also it gave them a secure belonging. Eicke weeded out those men he regarded not fit for concentration camp duty and only kept reliable, disciplined SS officers, NCOs, and enlisted men. As he expanded the camp system the commandant's SS cadre served him with devoted allegiance and fanaticism.

Promotions within the SS cadre were a common occurrence, especially among model SS.

His men knew that to progress further through the ranks they would have to strengthen their beliefs that all the prisoners detained inside the concentration camp system were inferior, and that they were implacable enemies of the state, against whom the SS were waging a war. They were aware that the slightest vestige of sympathy towards those in the concentration camps was regarded by the SS as intolerable. They had learnt to conceal any type of lingering feeling or compassion for those incarcerated and followed Eicke's doctrine of being 'hard'.

As inspector of concentration camps Eicke soon established a permanent concentration camp system that included notorious camps such as Sachsenhausen and Buchenwald. Eicke based Sachsenhausen on the Dachau model that he had created. The brutal methods of mistreating prisoners were applied in other camps, along with Dachau's harsh disciplinary and punishment regulations, which included the death penalty and punishment by the whip. As with Dachau, solitary confinement, general physical abuse and forced labour became standard practice.

The commandant of Sachsenhausen, *SS-Standartenführer* Baranowski was infused by Eicke with fanaticism and elitism. Like all Death Head members of the new *SS-Totenkopfbände* they were to be unfeeling to any type of human suffering. Baranowski's personnel looked upon him as a model commandant, whom they admired for being hard and mercilessly strict. Life at the Sachsenhausen camp was very similar to that of other concentration camps at that time, but under Baranowski's command there was a steady increase of brutality against the inmates and a rise in the death rate. The process of indoctrination of highly disciplined guards made Sachsenhausen a model camp.

By the late 1930s Nazi foreign policy became increasingly aggressive. Eicke made it clear to his men that the threat of war meant that the SS would expand to provide greater internal security, and that as a consequence the concentration camps would fill with new prisoners.

SS Reichsführer Heinrich Himmler had already envisaged an expansion programme, but this would not include Eicke. Eicke was allowed to retain command of the camps and the new *SS-Verfügungstruppe* (Special Service Troops), but all policy matters concerning the *Totenkopferbände* would be run at the highest level between Himmler and the *Führer*, Adolf Hitler.

With new government policies and with prospects of war against Poland looming, a more hostile attitude was instilled across the concentration camp system. There was even less tolerance towards the inmates and new slogans of hatred and discrimination were plastered around the camps for guards to read.

(*Above*) On 1 September 1939 the German Army unleashed its might against Poland. Here in this photograph is a column of armoured vehicles destined for the front lines.

(*Opposite page & following*) Four photographs showing SS-VT (later *Waffen-SS*) belonging to the *Leibstandarte* Adolf Hitler Division probably during action around the town of Sochaczew. Along the Bzura near Sochaczew there was heavy fighting between Hitler's foremost fighting machine and Polish forces. What followed after the battle were scenes of mass destruction. Columns of dead civilians, troops, cattle and horses had perished during intensive and prolonged attacks by the army and units of the *SS-Leibstandarte*, and were laid tangled inside ditches and clearings along the road leading to Warsaw.

A *Wehrmacht* unit on patrol inside a newly captured Polish town. Troops were often assigned to weed out resistance fighters and anyone they regarded as a threat to the German invasion. Behind the military arm of the SS-VT and the German Army lurked the SS Death's-Head groups or *Totenkopfverbande* under the notorious command of Theodor Eicke. Three regiments had been deployed in Poland: SS Oberbayern, Brandenburg, and Thuringen. Eicke's men quickly gained a reputation. In a matter of days they began torturing and killing Poles they regarded as being hostile to the Reich.

While the German war machine marched its way through Poland, troops came across eastern Jews for the first time. As the soldiers entered these towns, with their dreary buildings and hut-like dwellings, their unhealthy thoughts about the East were reinforced. They now got a firsthand view of the land which Germany was going to ruthlessly conquer. Among those walking along the dusty untended roads and going about their business were men in high-crowned hats and caftans. They had seen these figures in many of the anti-Semitic drawings plastered up on notice boards, walls and lamp-posts throughout Germany. They were the enemy, the Jews. For these German soldiers, protection of the *Reich* against such enemies was a priority. For some time it had become almost a religious creed to hate all Jews, especially those from the East.

Two portrait photographs of *Obergruppenführer* Theodor Eicke. Eicke had been made commander of Dachau concentration camp in June 1933 and had become a major figure in the SS. He was regarded as the architect, builder, and director of the concentration camp system and ruled it with an iron fist. As a man he was stocky in appearance, and gave off an aura of raw energy. Once the Germans had conquered Poland, Eicke acquired more freedom and power than ever before. The concentration camp system could now be expanded across Poland, and Eicke could infuse even more hatred against Jews and emigrants. As the Germans rounded up Jews and political prisoners, Eicke instructed his men to be brutal and use whatever violence necessary.

(*Opposite above*) SS training during the early part of the war. SS men who entered the realms of the concentration camp system saw the chance of joining an elite organisation with a strict system of beliefs and values based on military virtues of obedience and self-discipline.

(*Opposite below*) An SS training school. New recruits sought the idea of becoming part of this new order, not only because it was a racial-ideological elite, but for status reasons and also for the chance to become part of an organisation that looked likely to play a major role in Germany's path to recovery.

Regimental photograph at an SS training school. Many were attracted by the camaraderie of the SS, and were keen to broaden their career prospects in a military system that would become the major part of their life.

At an SS training school: recruits preparing to show how fit they are during a swimming exercise.

Here are two photographs showing recruits being sworn into the SS. These men had sworn an oath containing the words 'my loyalty is my honour'. They would have to prove their loyalty by doing any task assigned to them, even if it meant killing innocent men, women and children.

Seven photographs showing an SS training ground with soldiers seen on a parade ground in front of their commanding officers during what appears to be a passing out ceremony. The recruits learned about enemies of the state and were indoctrinated with the SS philosophy of racial superiority. These ideological teachings were aimed at producing men who ardently believed in the new Aryan order.

An SS marching band, probably during the fall of Paris in June 1940.

A photograph taken at an SS training ground showing troops on parade in front of their commanding officer.

Three more photographs at an SS training ground showing troops on parade in front of their commanding officers. At least three times a week these trainees had to listen to formal lectures covering policies of the Nazi Party, which included in-depth indoctrination into SS philosophy. The lectures covered many topics, and in particular the theories that the Aryan race was superior to those they regarded as sub-human, for example Slavs and Jews.

Three photographs showing a column of *Totenkopf* troops on horseback and on a foot march. At the outbreak of the Second World War, one of the first combat units of the *Waffen-SS*, the SS Division *Totenkopf* was formed from SS-TV personnel. It was the *SS-Totenkopfverbände* (SS-TV), Death's-Head Units, which were the SS organization responsible for administering the Nazi concentration camps, and were not connected in any way to the *Waffen-SS* arm of the *Totenkopf* Division.

(*Above*) *Totenkopf* recruits marching during a training exercise in 1939.

(*Opposite page* & *following*) Eight photographs showing men of the *SS-Totenkopf* during a funeral ceremony. Training in the SS-style was often hazardous, especially when the men were supplied with live ammunition during exercises. Such aggressive training led inevitably to fatalities, but the SS were firm believers in the 'train hard, fight easy' school. The training also made the average SS man much more willing to lay down his life in honour of *der Führer*. Off the battlefield the *Totenkopf* Division still had close ties to the concentration camp service and its members continued to wear the Death's-Head as their unit insignia. They were known for brutal tactics, a result of the original doctrine of no mercy which Eicke had instilled in his camp personnel during the thirties.

During a break in their training these SS men queue with their mess tins for soup.

SS troops pose for a group photograph during their training. As members of the SS these men were taught by their commandants to implement orders to the prisoners with horrific efficiency, in order to ensure that every officer, non-commissioned officer and SS guard was infused with the same brutal mentality as their commandant.

A photograph of Eicke with other commanding officers, in his role as inspector of the concentration camps. Eicke had begun an extensive reorganisation of the camps in 1935, with smaller camps being dismantled. Dachau camp remained, which was the first ever built, then Sachsenhausen opened in summer 1936, and Buchenwald in summer 1937. Dachau became the training centre for the concentration camps service. On 29 March 1936, the concentration camp guards and administration units were officially designated as the *SS-Totenkopfverbände* (*SS-TV*). Eicke's reorganisations and the introduction of forced labour camps were the SS's most powerful tools in the Third Reich. They earned Eicke a good reputation and total support from his *SS-Reichsführer*, Heinrich Himmler. *(USHMM 51639)*

The entrance to the SS compound at the infamous concentration camp, Mauthausen. Built in upper Austria, Mauthausen was greatly expanded over time, and by the summer of 1940 it had become one of the largest labour camp complexes in German-controlled Europe. Between 1939 and 1945 the camp was ruled with an iron fist by Franz Ziereis. By order of Eicke, Ziereis was quickly promoted to the rank of *SS-Sturmbannführer*, and on 20 April 1944 he received his final promotion to *SS-Standartenführer*.

Chapter Two

Road to Murder

Almost all of the SS commands as concentration camp commandants came from middle class backgrounds. Their fathers were often salesmen, shop owners and/or bank managers. The majority of them had finished secondary school, some had been privately schooled, some had been to university. Most were Nazi party members in the ranks of the SS or SA. Generally though, most were from a similar social background and were regarded as above average in the realms of the SS. They were generally posted across the concentration camp system because of their exceptional qualities or characteristics. Most of the staff were married and held no criminal record. In the main they knew what to expect: they were being sent to administer labour, concentration or death camps. But what is sinister is the fact that almost all kept their posting secret from their families and to other families. They reasoned that while they were on duty, whatever appalling acts they were performing, they were doing so under order and that they had to obey the law. Equally, they knew that they had a choice – either be posted to a concentration camp, or else fight on the battlefield with a military unit and face a high risk of death or injury. Also the commandants received special inducements for their work, such as extra pay, privileges for private schooling or tutors for their children, and rent free living, normally in the commandant's villa residence, which was often on site at the edge of the concentration camp.

Many had already bloodied their hands, and were somewhat accustomed to the tasks they would be performing. They looked upon their duties, however brutal or psychologically disturbing, merely as a job, and performed all their tasks hiding behind the facade that 'they were only following orders'. In this way they were able to exhibit cruelty towards their victims and think that they would somehow not be accountable for their actions. By blaming the system they believed they could do almost anything and need not feel a conscience.

A number of them had already used their own initiative to help devise methods by which to kill large numbers of people. Whilst in meetings with their staff they spoke openly without emotion about the killing of men, women, and children. The systematic murder of the Jews was a new order and they saw it as a new enterprise to be carried out with maximum efficiency: the creating of killing factories or work camps where they would work the inmates to death. It was a new concept; one which they hoped would bring bigger and better results, and brought brutality to a new level. The commandants knew the task ahead would not be without its difficulties, but they had sworn an oath with the motto, 'My loyalty is my honour'. They would have to prove their loyalty by doing the task which was given to them.

They were aware that their job was secret, and that their relatives, their friends, and their loved ones were not to be told anything about their job. Every SS man that came into the concentration camp system was determined from the outset to conceal as much of the gruesome knowledge as possible from the outside world. It was not just that they were being faithful to their oaths, but they were protecting their own credentials as human beings. In order to make it easier for them and lessen the physiological impact, they separated their families and loved ones from the gruesome tasks they performed. Once in their role they were able to embark on the mechanised extermination of literally hundreds of thousands of men, women, and children.

For the commandants being posted for the first time in a concentration camp there was no feeling of despondency or apprehension of what may be in store for them. They arrived at their new specially prepared quarters knowing that they had an important job to undertake. They had been trained in the teachings of Eicke, and followed his doctrine of being hard and ruthless. As if it were an industrial operation, they undertook wholesale murder by ensuring that the trains sent the victims on schedule and that the gas chambers worked in complete synchronization and could cope with the vast volumes of new arrivals.

The commandant of Auschwitz, Rudolf Höss, was no ruthless SS soldier like Eicke, who was both feared and revered by his men. Höss was a man who always appeared calm and collected and rarely openly denounced his enemies with anger or recrimination. For him it was not just a personal crusade to rid the world of the enemies of the state, as it was for Eicke and for other high ranking SS, but more a matter of an ardent desire to be part of the membership of a privileged order, such as the SS was, based on command and obedience. In the realms of the SS he was resolute in carrying out with maximum efficiency any orders laid down, no matter how brutal they were.

When Höss got his first command as commandant of Auschwitz in the spring of 1940 he never quite envisaged what his bosses had in store for him just two years later. The camp evolved from holding political prisoners to Jews. Unbeknown to the commandant, Auschwitz would soon be turned from a concentration camp to a murder and labour camp – the largest in the Nazi domain.

By the summer of 1941 Höss was given plans for an improved killing facility at the camp which would be capable of exterminating larger numbers of inmates. Since early summer Höss had been aware of growing plans to systematically murder prisoners at Auschwitz. Initially the condemned had been only the sick and disabled, now the *Reichsführer* Heinrich Himmler had decided on grander plans, to produce a factory-like killing installation that was capable of removing in large numbers those considered a threat to the *Reich* or those unfit for slave labour.

The first experiments of mass execution at the camp were with crystallized prussic acid, which was sold in tins marked with the name Zyklon B. Over 900 Russian prisoners were gassed using this new innovative method of systematic murder.

The gassing had been a complete success. No longer would the killers have to look into the eyes of their victims as they murdered them. Now they could transport their victims straight into a specially adapted gas chamber and have them killed all together, sparing, as Höss called it, a bloodbath. This new procedure appealed greatly to Höss. He found that with this innovation the new arrivals could quite easily be led into the crematorium not knowing they were going to be killed, but simply told they were to be disinfected by taking a shower. It had proven very easy to get inmates into the gas chamber by deception rather than using of force. This was all less stressful for the guards who were assigned to these murderous duties.

Höss expected more shipments of POWs to be killed in this manner, but his concern was now not the killing process, but the problems of storage and incineration of the corpses. These difficulties would soon be overcome by a new site constructed near the main camp of Auschwitz, called Birkenau.

Plans for a new crematorium had already been drawn up in late 1941, and it was expected to arrive very soon. Höss had found the perfect killing installation. The crematorium process at Auschwitz I had been inadequate; here at Birkenau he did not have the same disadvantages. Those unfit for work could now be taken away with ease, their death agonies would not disturb the local surroundings, and their bodies could be disposed of *en masse* and in secrecy.

Here at Birkenau the site would soon be able to house literally thousands of inmates, many of them Jews. In Höss's eyes the Jews who could work were a valuable resource. Those considered unfit for work would be sent to the specially erected gas chamber, and given 'special treatment'. Although Birkenau appeared to be the ideal solution for a vast slave labour pool, Höss had been aware for some weeks of newer harsher policies against the Jews. He also received reports that other camps in Poland were under construction near the villages of Belzec, Sobibor and Treblinka, which were to include their own crematoria as well. It appeared all Jews would be sent to these camps. The future for these hapless people looked bleaker than ever before.

Himmler's decree that the Jews were to be exterminated was in Höss's and all the commandants' minds, binding. After all, they had placed themselves in the phalanx of the SS and had been trained to blindly follow any orders given to them. Since the order had come down the command chain to murder the Jews many of the commandants had been at their most creative and imaginative, finding ways to help kill the prisoners on a larger scale using gas. These men who had been given the death camps to command had effectively become executives for the mass murder of Jews. For them, murder was to be an administrative procedure, and they assumed their mission of liquidating the Jews in a businesslike manner. They saw their positions like directors of corporations, managing the supply of raw materials to a factory, where they were monitored for quality and then processed through the plant. In front of their superiors they saw themselves as reliable obedient officers whose energy, determination and innovative skills would ensure that their camps were successful and effective killing factories.

A column of Pz.Kpfw.IIs roll through a Soviet town during the initial stages of the invasion of Russia. Looking on from the side of the road is a group of Jews, not knowing their fate in the hands of their invaders. The Nazis saw the Soviet Union as a land ripe for plunder and were determined to bring down the Soviet regime, destroy its army, murder those regarded hostile to the Reich, and to eliminate the Jews.

Five photographs showing a German police unit in the rear areas of the Soviet Union. When the Germans unleashed their attack against the Soviet Union on 22 June 1941, the Jewish problem escalated further. For the Nazi empire the prospect of a war against Russia entailed a transition from one policy of murder to another. This in effect brought into being the most radical ideas imaginable of the SS. As Hitler had explained to his generals a few months before the invasion, the war would be no normal war: it was an 'ideological war of extermination'. In the eyes of Hitler the Soviet Union represented the home of Bolshevism and of international Jewry, both of which needed to be rooted out and destroyed. To deal with the Jews in Russia, four *Einsatzgruppen* (Action Groups) were formed that consisted of *Sipo-SD* personnel, *Waffen-SS* units, and police.

A *Totenkopf* commanding officer during a presentation ceremony out in the field during combat operations in Russia. Progress through the Soviet heartlands was swift, and a blood bath against the Jewish population ensued.

A flak crew poses for the camera in the Russian winter of 1941. Although fighting stagnated along the Eastern Front, policies against the Soviet population and the Jews continued with unabated ferocity.

Six photographs showing Russian soldiers being captured by both SS and *Wehrmacht* forces. All over Russia, as the Germans advanced deeper into the Soviet heartlands, ruthless actions against Russian Jews, Communist politicians and political commissars continued. In Poland, concentration camps that had been erected all over the country were made ready to receive these Russian POWs. Many of them never arrived at their designated camps: they were either murdered by firing squad, starved to death in the POW holding camps, or died en-route on death marches to Poland. Conditions for the Soviet prisoners were appalling.

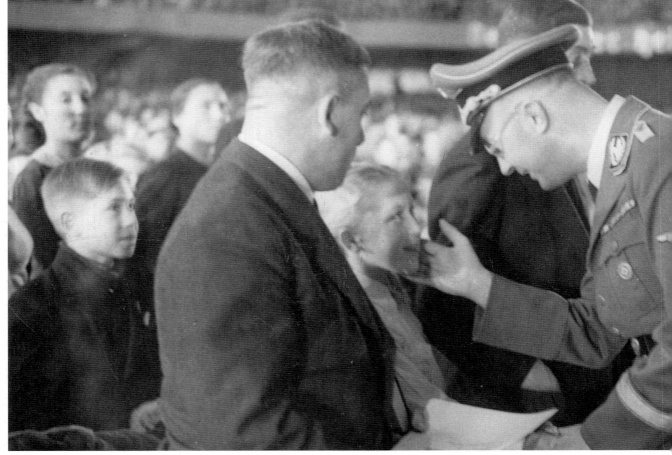

(*Above*) An SS sentry box with SS guards outside an administration building.

(*Opposite above*) At a luncheon Hitler sits with his commanding officers. By this period the German war machine was invading Russia and it seemed it would soon defeat the Soviet enemy. In conquered Poland the Poles were already experiencing what the Nazis intended to inflict on the Russians. Throughout the country there was more or less unrestrained terror, particularly in the incorporated territories. The area not incorporated, with a population of some eleven million, consisted of the Polish province of Lublin and parts of the provinces of Warsaw and Krakow, and was named the 'General Government'. This large area became the dumping ground for all undesirables and those deemed enemies of the State. It was to here that the first deportations of Poles and Jews were sent in their thousands. In the General Government the Germans created ghettos where they could contain the Jews before they were transported direct to one of the many new concentration camps being constructed.

(*Opposite below*) *SS-Reichsführer* Heinrich Himmler was known as the architect of genocide. In this photograph he feebly touches the cheek of a young German child. Behind this façade Himmler was already putting into effect the wholesale liquidation of the Jewish population.

Two photographs showing a typical SS mess, complete with bunk and SS insignia plastered across the walls. Generally the barracks and mess was where most of the personnel spent their time, eating, drinking and playing cards. For these men, however callous and evil some of them were, they felt that the confines of these buildings were a kind of sanctuary from their daily duty of killing and torturing.

An interesting photograph showing an SS and *Wehrmacht* soldier smiling with two concentration camp officials in the General Government of Poland at Christmas 1942. The original caption reads 'camp official brothers with their fighting comrades at Christmas in Poland 1942'.

A portrait photograph of a member of the *SS-Totenkopf* wearing his field cap with infamous death head badge.

Members of the *Totenkopf* drinking and relaxing in their mess.

A group photograph showing members of the *Totenkopf*, probably during the early winter of 1942 on the Eastern Front.

A portrait photograph of *SS-Obersturmbannführer* Adolf Eichmann – a Jewish emigration specialist who had been given the task of facilitating and managing the logistics of mass deportations of Jews to ghettos and concentration camps in Nazi-occupied Eastern Europe.

Four photographs showing the deportation of Jews probably during the winter of 1942. At the Wannsee conference held in Berlin in January 1942, Nazi officials gathered to consider the fate of the Jewish population. With many of the concentration camps already constructed it was agreed that it would be the Jews in the General Government of Poland who would be dealt with first. The Nazi leadership was under no illusion that it would require all of their organisational skills to bring about mass murder on the scale they intended. Already a pool of experts had been drafted in to undertake this mammoth task and plans for death camps had already been proposed.

(*Above*) A photograph of Auschwitz camp commandant Rudolf Höss, seen standing in the middle of a delegation of Nazi officials that has visited the camp. Within three years of becoming commandant Höss had turned previously quiet and secluded Auschwitz into the largest mass murder factory in the history of the world. As commandant he had the entire camp under his control, and was only ever answerable to his superiors in Berlin. Like all other concentration camp commandants he had more or less unlimited power. He would issue orders daily to his officers, who would in turn read out these orders to the prisoners during their morning roll call. Höss normally gave written orders direct to his subordinates, and would supervise a particular department if he were required to. It was normally down to the commandant to issue punishments to any SS man that broke the rules in the camp, and could at any time have a member of staff replaced. (*Auschwitz Birkenau Museum*)

(*Opposite above*) A recent photograph taken of the old SS barracks outside the Auschwitz II camp, or Birkenau. (*HITM, courtesy of Auschwitz Birkenau Museum*)

(*Opposite above*) This recent photograph shows the main road running along the Birkenau camp from the SS barracks. Note the wooden watch towers along the perimeter of the camp. (*HITM, courtesy of Auschwitz Birkenau Museum*)

(*Above*) A rear view of the Höss villa showing how enclosed the garden was from the main camp. It was not unusual for officers and their families to be assigned houses like this. Throughout the summer and early autumn of 1942 at Auschwitz many officers and their families were housed either in the centre of the town or in the immediate vicinity of the main camp. They all enjoyed a far more comfortable lifestyle than any they could have achieved fighting on the frontline. It soon became a close-knit community where wives would visit each other, gossip, hold afternoon tea parties, and invite their husbands along for evening drinks and dinner. As for the children they would either attend private schools in Kattowitz and surrounding areas, or privately hire a governess. When the children were not attending school, they were looked after by domestic slaves who cooked meals and cleaned their nicely furnished homes. Initially a great number of servants employed were Polish prisoners, but many German families thought that the Poles were too inferior to make good servants, or else they were worried they might try to attack them. (*HITM, courtesy of Auschwitz Birkenau Museum*)

(*Opposite page*) Two recent photographs taken by the author of camp commandant Rudolf Höss's residence at Auschwitz, commonly known as the Höss villa. The house was an imposing two storey stucco building situated in the north-eastern corner of the camp. The front of the building, with its large windows and small terrace, overlooked the Rajsko to Auschwitz road (seen here with the author's friend Kevin Bowden and Polish taxi driver and guide Halina Kapka). There was a little garden to the front with a small brick wall and gate to the main entrance to the house. To the side of the building there was a double gate with a drive where vehicles could access the property. On the opposite side of the house, reached by a concrete path, was the tradesman's entrance, which consisted of a flight of concrete steps leading to the side door with a porch, which overlooked the garden. The garden itself was predominantly situated to the side of the house and consisted of a number of trees and shrubs from the previous occupants. A fence with barbed wire was erected around the perimeter of the garden and the house, in order to divide it from the main camp. In November 1942 a new high concrete fencing was constructed and topped with barbed wire to replace the old fencing around the entire boundary of the camp. The new fencing was also installed at the rear and the sides of the Höss villa, making the house completely separated from the camp and virtually invisible from the garden, except for the roofs and chimneys of the Commandant's office and administration buildings. The fence to the rear of the house, which hid the Commandant's office, administration offices, SS guardhouse and the newly constructed crematorium, was further hidden by a large mound of earth placed behind the fence, and trees planted. Höss had been particularly insistent on trying to conceal the villa from the camp as much as possible, and made it known that he wanted his family to live in absolute privacy. (*HITM, courtesy of Auschwitz Birkenau Museum*)

(*Above*) A recent photograph taken from within the compound of Auschwitz main camp, showing on the left some of the brick buildings that housed prisoners, ringed by an electric fence and overlooked by a watch tower. Note behind the watch tower, the 'Höss villa'. (*HITM, courtesy of Auschwitz Birkenau Museum*)

(*Opposite above*) A recent photograph showing the commandant's office at Auschwitz main camp. This rather large imposing brick building generally dealt with matters that affected the SS staff. It was primarily responsible for keeping all records and for supplying the garrison with weapons and other important military equipment. All transport and communications were controlled from this office. The office was divided into a number of different sections which included: Office Supply, Communications Office, Judicial Affairs, Weapons, Military Supplies, and the Engineers Office. Each morning, camp commandant Rudolf Höss would walk across to Department I, the Commandant's office, and would converse with his office secretaries, answer any urgent messages or telegrams, and issue his daily written orders to his subordinates. The letters, telegrams, various telephone call messages and other paper work that were classed not as urgent were regularly taken home to be dealt with in his study. When he was not in his office or at home in his study, he was often seen strolling in the camp, ensuring that everything was being run efficiently. He would converse with officers, making sure commands were being adhered to. (*HITM, courtesy of Auschwitz Birkenau Museum*)

(*Opposite below*) Here a recent photograph shows one of the main debarkation areas for unloading Jews by train, mainly Hungarian, in the summer of 1944. It was intended that many Hungarian Jews were to be transported to Auschwitz where they would be selected for slave labour. Once they arrived at Birkenau, the Germans would separate those Jews who could serve the German war effort through work, and those unfit for labour, including children and their mothers, who would be immediately sent to the gas chambers and murdered. Adolf Eichmann was in charge of transporting the Hungarian Jews directly to Auschwitz, and negotiated with the Hungarian police, who helped organise the so-called ghettoisation of the Jewish population in Hungary. Whilst plans had been put into place to select the Hungarian Jews for slave labour when they arrived at Birkenau, many in fact were simply sent straight to the gas chambers in what the camp commandant called 'special treatment'. Almost 350,000 Hungarians were murdered over the course of several weeks in the summer of 1944. (*HITM, courtesy of Auschwitz Birkenau Museum*)

A recent photograph showing the infamous rail line in Birkenau. This line was built mainly for the sole purpose of transporting Hungarian Jews direct to the camp. The first major Hungarian transports steamed their way through to Auschwitz on 15 May 1944. Once they arrived, the train pulled over the new spur through the gate into Birkenau and halted at the ramps. Here at the ramps 'Aktion Höss', as it was known, was put into operation. First, the Jews were unloaded from the cattle cars. Next, they were separated into two columns, one of women and children; the other of men. A selection was then carried out by one or two SS medical doctors, and the two columns were divided into four columns: two of women and children, and two of men. Those unfit for labour were sent straight ahead toward the crematoria, whilst all able-bodied workers were interned in Auschwitz, or were retained ready at a moment's notice to be transferred to other camps in the *Reich*. The selection for labour in each transport varied daily. Sometimes it was as low as 10 per cent, sometimes as high as 50 per cent. But the majority of Jews who arrived through the gates of Birkenau were quickly sent through to the 'bathhouses' to their deaths. There were roughly 3,300 people per day arriving, sometimes that figure rising to 4,300. (*HITM, courtesy of Auschwitz Birkenau Museum*)

A recent photograph showing the furnace in the former powder magazine store in Auschwitz I. This store was first modified to be used for delousing purposes, but was modified again in the summer of 1940 and turned into a crematorium for the incineration of prisoners who died in the camp. Before the crematorium was in operation those who died were transported to Gliwice and incinerated in the municipal crematorium. The installation was undertaken by J.A. Topf and Sons of Erfurt, a company with a section specialising in the manufacture and installation of crematorium furnaces, headed by chief engineer Kurt Prüfer. In order to conceal the crematorium from view a one-storey building housing the SS hospital was constructed nearby, along with the camp workshops and the barracks of the political department. By late 1940 or early 1941 the crematoria were becoming overworked with the large numbers being killed inside the camp or dying from disease. By this period further plans were being considered for the disposal of the dead. Early on in Auschwitz corpses were buried in mass pits or burned on huge outside fire incinerators. Once Birkenau had been built and the huge crematoria erected, this generally alleviated the problems of mass corpse disposal. (*HITM, courtesy of Auschwitz Birkenau Museum*)

(*Above*) A photograph taken in the summer of 1944 showing (from left to right) Rudolf Höss, *SS-Hauptsturmführer* Josef Kramer, and *SS-Obersturmführer* Anton Thumann. In May 1944, roughly when this photograph was taken, Kramer was put in charge of the gas chambers in Auschwitz. He was to hold that position until December 1944, when he was transferred and appointed as Commandant of Belsen. As For Anton Thumann, he had been Protective Custody Camp Leader at the Majdanek concentration camp and was known by the prisoners as the 'Hangman of Majdanek'. At the time of this photograph he had been appointed Protective Custody Camp Leader at Neuengamme concentration camp, a position he held until the end of the war. (*Courtesy of USHMM Archives*)

(*Opposite above*) A group of SS officers gather in front of a building at Solahütte, the SS retreat outside Auschwitz. From left to right are Josef Kramer, Dr Josef Mengele, Richard Baer, Karl Hocker and Walter Schmidetzki, *SS-Sturmbannführer* and commander of Auschwitz I from May 1944 to February 1945. *SS-Obersturmführer* Karl Hocker was adjutant to Richard Baer. As for *SS-Hauptsturmführer* Dr Josef Mengele, he had won the Iron Cross 1st Class and was the most highly decorated SS officer at Auschwitz. He had volunteered to come to Auschwitz to establish an experimental physiology and pathology department. After his arrival it was not long before he was revelling in his power to carry out his extreme ideas without mercy. (*Courtesy of USHMM archives*)

(*Opposite below*) SS officers at an unknown railway terminal stand in front of cattle cars similar to those used for transporting Jews to the concentration camps. The seizure and deportation of thousands of Jews to the concentration camps had not been an easy task. There had been problems with rail lines and railcars moving across Europe to the East and the unexpected military setbacks on the Eastern Front had represented a number of difficult circumstances for the rolling stock. But the Nazis were determined that the war would not influence the successful outcome of the 'Final Solution'.

At an unknown location two SS men are seen being given their rations from a mobile kitchen. These mobile kitchens were used extensively by both *Wehrmacht* and *Waffen-SS* troops on the front lines. They were also used at camps under construction where kitchens had not yet been built.

A portrait of *SS-Sturmbannführer* Arthur Liebehenschel. On 1 December 1943, he was appointed commandant of Auschwitz, succeeding Rudolf Höss. When Höss returned to Auschwitz, Liebehenschel was replaced as commandant on 8 May 1944 and appointed commandant of the Majdanek extermination camp on 19 May 1944, succeeding Martin Gottfried Weiss.

(*Left*) A photograph of *SS-Hauptsturmführer* Hans Bothmann. Bothmann was the last commandant of the Chelmno extermination camp from 1942, and commander of the SS Special Detachment. Bothmann was responsible for the extermination of Jews from the Lodz Ghetto. He was able to boast that Chelmno had murdered 180,000 Jews from the summer of 1942 until the camp was finally closed in March 1943. Bothmann was dispatched to Yugoslavia, but a year later he was summoned back to Poznań to command a renewed killing operation at Chelmno. In this final phase of the camp operation some 25,000 victims were murdered under the supervision of Bothmann. However, with the continued deportation of Jews from the East and other victims regarded as hostile to the Reich, in mid-July 1944 the SS and police began deporting the remaining inhabitants of the Lodz ghetto to Auschwitz for immediate destruction. (*Courtesy of M. Kaldow*)

(*Right*) *SS-Standartenführer* Arthur Hermann Florstedt. He initially served at Sachsenhausen concentration camp from 1940 until 1942 when he was transferred to Majdanek extermination camp to replace *SS-Sturmbannführer* Max Koegel. Florstedt ruled the camp with an iron fist from October 1942. However, later in the war he was replaced by the interim commander Martin Gottfried Weiss after the SS charged Florstedt with embezzlement and widespread stealing. In fact, many commandants found it tempting to steal and sell their goods on the black market. The camps were literally a treasure trove to members of the SS. They had seen nothing like it before, and many of them were unable to resist the temptation provided by these 'riches'. Supervision was surprisingly slack and as a result many actively participated in theft. Stealing and corruption was rife amongst the SS in the camps, and the black market thrived. Many of the commandants personally benefitted. Diamonds, gold, coins, dollars, and foreign currency from all over Europe were stolen. Large amounts of food and alcohol too were taken for personal use and sold on the black market. Items of clothing and furniture were also pilfered by the SS, benefitting from the dead.

A photograph taken in the summer of 1941 showing SS officers in Gross-Rosen bidding farewell to SS platoon Commander Hafer who was responsible for the building. Gross-Rosen was constructed in the summer of 1940 as a satellite camp of the Sachsenhausen complex. In May 1941 it became an independent slave labour camp with prisoners being forced to work in a huge stone quarry owned by the *SS-Deutsche Erd- und Steinwerke GmbH* (SS-German Earth and Stone Works). *(USHMM 55776, provenance: Martin Mansson)*

SS man Papka poses with two puppies in the Gross-Rosen concentration camp. At its peak of activity in 1944, the Gross-Rosen complex had around 100 sub-camps. Almost 130,000 various nationalities, including Soviet POWs, were sent to the complex as slave labourers. Some 40,000 people died there. *(USHMM 55790)*

(*Above*) The commander of Gross-Rosen, *SS-Obersturmbannführer* Arthur Rödl sits at his desk in his office with a photograph of Adolf Hitler hanging on the wall. (*USHMM 36214, provenance: Martin Mansson*)

(*Opposite page*) *SS-General* Oswald Pohl pays an official visit to Auschwitz, accompanied by Auschwitz Commandant Richard Baer who had previously served as his adjutant. Pohl oversaw the organisation of the concentration camps system, and was responsible for deciding which detainees would be transported to the various camps for slave labour. In the summer of 1944 Pohl also directed the management of the extermination of the Hungarian Jews at Auschwitz. (*USHMM 34591*)

(*Above*) SS officers supervising the building of a gallows in the forest near the Buchenwald concentration camp. (*USHMM 13138, courtesy of Robert A. Schmuhl*)

(*Opposite above*) Jews from the Lodz ghetto board deportation trains for the Chelmno death camp. The camp operated from 8 December 1941 to March 1943 during *Aktion Reinhard*, and from June 1944 to 18 January 1945. Its primary function was to exterminate Jews of the Lodz Ghetto and the local Polish inhabitants in surrounding areas. (*USHMM 02625, courtesy of National Museum of American Jewish History*)

(*Opposite below*) Commandant Franz Ziereis points out something to *SS-Reichsführer* Heinrich Himmler and other SS officials while viewing the quarry during an inspection tour of the Mauthausen concentration camp. Pictured in front, from left to right, are: Heinrich Himmler, Franz Ziereis and Ernst Kaltenbrunner. To the right of Kaltenbrunner is Josef Kiermaier. (*USHMM 12059, courtesy of Archiv der KZ-Gedenkstaette Mauthausen*)

(*Above*) View of the moat in front of the barbed wire fence surrounding the Dachau concentration camp. (*USHMM 75040, courtesy of William and Dorothy McLaughlin*)

(*Opposite above*) SS guards supervise the arrival of a transport of Jews from Subcarpathian Rus to Auschwitz-Birkenau. Pictured on the far right is *SS-Wachmann* Stefan Baretzki. During the Frankfurt trials (1963–1965) this photograph was used as evidence against Baretzki. (*USHMM 77414, courtesy of Yad Vashem*)

(*Opposite below*) Deportation of Jews from the Lodz ghetto to the Chelmno death camp between January and March 1942. (*USHMM 83503, courtesy of Yad Vashem Photo Archives*)

(*Above*) Commandant Franz Ziereis poses with members of the SS staff of the Mauthausen concentration camp. From left to right are *Hauptsturmführer* Erich Wasitzky (the camp apothecary); Karl Schulz, chief of 'Politischer Abteilung' (Gestapo office in the camp); *Standartenführer* Franz Ziereis (the camp commandant); *Sturmbannführer* Eduard Krebsbach (camp doctor); Karl Boehmichen (camp doctor) and an unidentified *Obersturmführer*. (*USHMM 06440, courtesy of Eugene S. Cohen*)

(*Opposite above*) High ranking SS officials on an inspection tour of the Mauthausen concentration camp. Pictured in the front row, from left to right, are Ernst Kaltenbrunner, Franz Ziereis, Heinrich Himmler, Karl Chmielewski, and August Eigruber. At the far right in the second row is George Bachmayer. (*USHMM 12057, courtesy of Instytut Pamieci Narodowej*)

(*Opposite below*) Commandant Franz Ziereis accompanies Heinrich Himmler on an inspection tour of the Mauthausen concentration camp. Heinrich Himmler is pictured second from the right. Behind him is Franz Ziereis, the Commandant of Mauthausen. (*USHMM 66700, courtesy of David Mendels*)

Chapter Three

Reinhard Camp Commandants

The killing success of the camps was of paramount importance to the commandants, so much so in fact that the commandant of Auschwitz, Rudolf Höss decided to journey by train to a recently built concentration camp called Treblinka in the summer of 1942 to see for himself a fully operational death camp. The camp was situated fifty miles northeast of Warsaw on the main Warsaw-Bialystok railway line near the quiet village of Treblinka.

At the gas chambers where Höss was supposed to seek inspiration he observed the killing process, and was not very impressed. He wrote that 'small gas chambers, equipped with pipes to induce the exhaust gas from the engines, coming from old captured transport vehicles and tanks, very often failed to work. Because of that the intakes could not be dealt with according to the plan, which meant to clear the Warsaw ghetto. According to the camp commandant of Treblinka 80,000 people have been gassed in the course of half a year.' In Höss's view Treblinka was not a very efficient camp. His gas chambers at Auschwitz were much larger, and unlike Treblinka he would not waste valuable resources and time killing Jews with exhaust gas. The victims too that arrived at Treblinka knew their fate, whilst at Auschwitz Höss could boast that the victims were fooled into believing they were going through a delousing process.

Following Höss's visit to Treblinka, Jews from all over Europe including Slovakia, France, Belgium and the Netherlands, men, women and children, were herded through into Birkenau like cattle and sent to their deaths. Yet in the midst of this horror Auschwitz during this period was still playing only a minor part in the slaughter of the Jews. The major killings were already established in the forests of Poland – Belzec, Sobibor and Treblinka.

Here in Treblinka, *Obersturmführer* Dr Irmfried Eberl, who had become the camp's first commandant, had a restless craving for power, and an ambition to achieve the highest possible numbers of gassed victims and exceed all the other camps. The commandant indeed delivered his bosses an exceptional killing rate, but the way he organised the camp led to his dismissal. The killing process was chaotic, and this chaos led to SS-men who did not normally have a tendency to cause pain and misery on the prisoners, to suddenly become habitually cruel. In the higher reaches of the SS, they wanted Eberl prosecuted for not organising the mass murder of men, women, and children in a more effective way. In the eyes of his superiors Eberl's crime was that he had not committed the crime of mass murder well enough.

After Eberl's departure the camp was transformed by the new commandant *SS-Hauptsturmführer* Franz Stangl, an old Austrian graduate of Hartheim 'euthanasia' centre. Stangl was determined to reform the camp and the SS that served there. He preached the need for rooting from the ranks the disobedient, the unreliable, and the lazy. He was determined to enforce the SS concepts of elitism, toughness, and comradeship, and imposed a ruthless discipline upon his subordinates, meting out harsh and often brutal punishments for the slightest infractions of SS rules.

In other death camps, such as Belzec, Christian Wirth, commander of the camp, ruled the camp by fear and terror. Wirth had arrived at Belzec before Christmas 1941, bringing with him a group of about ten 'euthanasia' specialists, including the notorious chemist, Dr Kallmeyer. They had been given the task of constructing a special gassing facility and to operate it. Killing people with the use of gas was not unknown to Wirth. In 1939 he became involved in the euthanasia actions against the mentally ill and assisted in the wholesale extermination of the victims using bottled carbon monoxide. Two years later in 1941 he was dispatched to Lublin where he continued his sadistic killings. Wirth soon earned himself a reputation and was nicknamed 'savage Christian'. At Belzec Wirth encouraged his SS personnel to commit terrible acts of brutality against their victims.

Within months of his arrival Wirth was adapting previous killing techniques with the use of gas. By February 1942 two gassing tests were undertaken at Belzec, the first with Zyklon B (hydrogen cyanide gas) and the second with bottled carbon monoxide. Among the victims of the second test were German-Jewish psychiatric patients deported from Germany and local Jews from Piaski and Izbica. As a cheaper alternative a Soviet tank engine was installed outside the chambers to produce carbon monoxide from exhaust gas which was fed into the chamber. The technique was a success and there was now no need for a constant supply of CO gas to a far distant part of Poland.

Wirth realised that because the vast majority of arrivals would be alive only for a matter of a few hours a large complex of wooden and concrete buildings, such as those found at Auschwitz would no longer be required. A death camp, unlike a concentration camp, needed only a few facilities to operate effectively. Wirth wanted to conceal the true purpose of the place from the new arrivals for as long as possible. So within the camp he had the gas chamber building camouflaged and hidden behind trees and a wire fence. He knew that by building a large gas chamber the killing process would not only spare his own men psychological suffering, but more importantly mean fewer personnel would be required to run the camp. He would employ a number of healthy Jewish slave labourers who would be selected upon arrival to the camp and put to work burying bodies, sorting the large quantities of clothing and valuables, and cleaning the gas chambers.

The Belzec death camp finally began its operations on 17 March 1942 with a transport of some fifty goods wagons containing Jews from Lublin. Between March and the end of April, thousands of Jews from the Lublin and Lemberg districts were successfully exterminated in Belzec. Himmler sent his congratulations to Wirth who had finally built a killing factory capable of murdering many hundreds of thousands of people in one single space. But Belzec alone would not be sufficient to deal with the numbers of people scheduled to be sent there.

In March while the first trainloads of Jews were being readied for Belzec, another 'Reinhard' death camp was being constructed. It was near the small village of Sobibor in a wooded area on the Chelmno-Wlodawa railway line a few miles south of Wlodawa. The installation was an enlarged and improved version of Belzec with the same general layout. *SS-Hauptsturmführer* Franz Stangl, who would later become commandant of Treblinka, was appointed commandant.

By the time Stangl received his new appointment Wirth had become commander of both Chelmno and Belzec, and was soon to oversee Stangl's operation at Sobibor.

Stangl was shocked by the first gassing and was determined that he would try to avoid the graphic spectacle in future. When Sobibor officially became operational in mid-May 1942, he did just that. 'At Sobibor', he said, 'one could avoid seeing almost all of it – it all happened so far away from the camp buildings.' Yet, in spite in Stangl's sensitivities about the camp operations it nonetheless accelerated its activities at tremendous pace. Within the first two months, some 100,000 people were killed there.

By the summer of 1942, both Sobibor and Belzec were running simultaneously, and despite the technical problems of machinery breaking down and the problems with body disposal, the 'Reinhard' camps were achieving what they had been intended for: the wholesale mass extermination of the Jews.

Two photographs of Reinhard Heydrich, *SS-Obergruppenführer* and *General der Polizei*, chief of the Reich Main Security Office, and *Stellvertretender Reichsprotektor* (Deputy/Acting Reich-Protector) of Bohemia and Moravia. It was on 20 January 1942 that Heydrich chaired the Wannsee Conference in Berlin, in which he revealed his dark plan to deport and transport 11 million Jews from all over Europe to where they would be forced into labour or destroyed in special extermination camps.

(*Left*) A photograph of *SS-Oberstgruppenführer* Odilo Globocnik. It was at the Wannsee Conference in Berlin that a special organization, later named 'Operation Reinhard', was established in Lublin. Operation Reinhard was the code name given for the systematic annihilation of the Polish Jews in the General Government, and it would mark the beginning of the most deadly phase of the programme: the use of extermination camps. The SS and Police Leader of the district of Lublin, *SS-Oberstgruppenführer* Odilo Globocnik, was appointed the commander of the operation. Globocnik was a ruthless and fanatical SS officer who believed wholeheartedly in the Nazi vision. From his office he planned and gossiped with his associates about the future SS colonization of the East and the task of preparing the extermination of Jews in the General Government. In order to undertake such an action against the Jews, killing centres were to be established. Globocnik set to work immediately. He brought in people who had been assigned to the euthanasia programme and had the knowledge and experience of setting up and operating factories for mass murder. Plans to construct three death camps were put forward, at Belzec, Sobibor, and Treblinka.

(*Right*) *SS-Sturmbannführer* Christian Wirth. In 1939 Wirth became involved in the euthanasia actions against the mentally ill and assisted in their wholesale extermination using bottled carbon monoxide. Two years later in 1941 he was dispatched to Lublin where he continued his sadistic killings. Wirth soon earned himself a reputation and was nicknamed 'savage Christian'. At Belzec concentration camp Wirth ruled the camp with an iron fist and encouraged his SS personnel to commit terrible acts of brutality against its inmates. Within months of his arrival Wirth was adapting previous killing techniques with the use of gas. By February 1942 two gassing tests were undertaken at Belzec, the first with Zyklon B (hydrogen cyanide gas), the second with bottled carbon monoxide. Among the victims of the second test were German-Jewish psychiatric patients deported from Germany, and local Jews from Piaski and Izbica. As a cheaper alternative, a Soviet tank engine was installed outside the chambers to produce carbon monoxide from exhaust gas which was fed into the chamber. The technique was a complete success and there was now no need for a constant supply of CO gas to this distant part of Poland.

(*Left*) A German newspaper photograph of *SS-Obersturmführer* Richard Thomalla. The contractors assigned to build Treblinka death camp were the German construction firms Schönbronn of Leipzig and Schmidt-Münstermann. These firms were to receive their commissions from the Central Construction Office of the *Waffen-SS* and Police in Warsaw. In charge of construction was *SS-Obersturmführer* Richard Thomalla, who had completed the building contract at Sobibor and had been replaced there by Stangl in April 1942. For almost eight weeks Thomalla and his subordinates oversaw the construction of Treblinka. The bulk of the labour force to build the installation was Jews, who were transported there by trucks from the neighboring villages of Wegrow and Stoczek Wegrowski. There were also a number of Poles used from the nearby labour camp Treblinka I. *SS-Untersturmführer* Heinz Auerswald from the office of the commissioner of the Warsaw ghetto supplied much of the construction materials.

(*Right*) *SS-Hauptsturmführer* Gottlieb Hering served in Action T4 Euthanasia Programme and later as the second and last commandant of Belzec extermination camp during Operation Reinhard.

(*Above*) Two photographs showing off-duty SS guards posing for the camera during the summer months of 1942. For these men mass murder became a fixture in their daily routine. Being subjected constantly to camp life hardened their conscience. Many regularly watched the shipments of Jews arriving and became morbidly fascinated by the spectacle. Outwardly the SS men showed no compassion whatsoever. They just looked on with a cold indifference watching the processions going to their death, hoping that the gassing process would not cause additional problems. Perhaps for them, killing by gas was easier to deal with psychologically than murdering men, women and children face-to-face. Gassing meant that they did not have to look into the eyes of their victims as they were killed.

(*Opposite page*) An SS officer with his wife poses for a portrait photograph. The original photograph was found in a small collection of artifacts in Poland near Sobibor, and it is presumed this unidentified man had a connection with the camp.

(*Above*) A photograph of *SS-Oberscharführer* Kurt Franz's St Bernard dog called Barry. Franz was deputy commander at Treblinka death camp. It did not take long before Franz made his mark at Treblinka, and soon became one of the most dominant SS men in the camp. To the prisoners he was one of the cruelest and frightening figures there. He was nicknamed 'Lalke' (doll in Yiddish) owing to his baby face. Often he would be seen riding on his horse touring the camp, visiting the work sites in the Lower camp and the extermination area. When he was not roaming the camp he took part in roll calls and the meting out of harsh punishments on the prisoners. He was also seen with his dog, Barry. Barry had been trained by Franz to be ferocious, and upon his command would attack Jews, biting at their bodies and sinking his sharp teeth into the victim's genitals, occasionally ripping them off. (*H.E.A.R.T*)

(*Opposite page*) Two photographs taken of the Treblinka excavator. The excavator had been brought over from Treblinka I and was used every day to dig corpse pits and help bury the dead. The excavator was built by Menck & Hambrock, type 'Ma', produced between 1933 and 1944, power: 70 HP, weight: 27 tons. These photos were taken by Stangl's deputy Kurt Franz. In one photograph two SS-men can be seen on the buckets of the excavator. These photographs were probably taken in the first half of 1943. At least two types of excavator were used in Treblinka: bucket and cable excavators. It was later realised that the bucket excavator was not very effective for digging burial pits. The photos were found in Franz's Treblinka album which he named *Schöne Zeiten* (Pleasant Times). (*ARC*)

A posed photograph of the first commandant of Treblinka, *SS-Obersturmführer* Dr Irmfried Eberl. As soon as Eberl took command he was determined to deliver an exceptional killing rate that far outweighed that of any other camp in the Nazi empire. (*H.E.A.R.T*)

A photograph of *SS-Hauptsturmführer* Franz Paul Stangl, dressed in his familiar white tunic and holding an oxhide whip, seen with his deputy Franz at Treblinka death camp. Stangl had earned a good reputation in the realms of the concentration camp system and was commandant of the Sobibor and Treblinka extermination camps during the Operation Reinhard phase. *(ARC)*

This photo was taken in August 1942 when Pötzinger visited the Treblinka cook August Hengst and his wife Augusta in Warsaw. During an interrogation after the war, Hengst talked about this visit. He was allowed to wear civilian clothes and had an apartment in Warsaw where he often welcomed visitors from Treblinka. At this time Hengst was busy getting food and other goods for the Treblinka camp staff. From time to time he had to travel to Treblinka. One day, camp commander Stangl forbade the wearing of civilian clothes. However, when Pötzinger and Pinnemann were on a visit, they decided to go to a photographic studio in the same road, where this photo was taken. *(ARC)*

(*Above*) A photograph taken at Treblinka showing an ammunition storeroom. It was located between the two SS barracks, and built during the first phase of the camp as a concrete cube. In spring 1943 a second storey was added, containing a water tank to supply new showers for the SS staff. During the revolt at Treblinka, the SS barracks burned down. This photo was taken by Kurt Franz, after the revolt. (*ARC*)

(*Opposite page*) A photograph showing the zoo at Treblinka death camp. At Treblinka, commandant Stangl had a zoo constructed near the Ukrainian barracks, in the early summer of 1943. Here the SS spent their leisure time sitting on wooden benches and tables relaxing and enjoying looking at the animals. (*ARC*)

An aerial view taken during an Allied reconnaissance mission over Poland in 1944, showing the former site of the Treblinka death camp. (ARC)

A group of SS men pose for the camera during 'Operation Reinhard' in the summer of 1942. These men were not assigned their tasks because of any exceptional qualities they had. Their anti-Semitism was part of their culture that had been nurtured over years of intense propaganda. Most were married, and the majority did not have a criminal record. They had volunteered to serve in the SS in a death camp where they carried out their duties loyally and unquestioningly and would show terrible cruelty toward their victims. When they were not physically or mentally abusing the prisoners, they were killing them, sometimes in their thousands each day.

(*Above*) Three SS men pose for the camera. The men who were posted to Treblinka wrote about their personal experiences as if they were 'normal'. They believed that their daily lives were predominantly very good.

Another photograph showing the same SS men. Although they were massively influenced by the propaganda of the times, it is evident they made a series of personal choices. They carried on working at Treblinka not just because they were ordered to, but because a posting to a concentration camp meant they would avoid the risks to life and limb associated with fighting on a battlefield in southern Russia. There is no record of any member of the SS refusing on moral grounds to work in the camp. They could have easily rejected the posting and got sent to the front, but all preferred to live a life in the camp, killing those they regarded as having no intrinsic right to life.

SS-Oberscharführer Kurt Franz, who had been appointed as deputy commandant at Treblinka. Before the war Franz had joined the 3rd *Waffen-SS-Totenkopfstandarte Thüringen*, and then later at the end of 1939 was summoned to the *Führer*'s Chancellery and detailed for service as cook in the euthanasia institutes at Grafeneck, Hartheim, Sonnenstein and Brandenburg. As a member of the 6th battalion he served at the Buchenwald concentration camp in 1941, and by the spring of 1942 had been ordered to the General Government where he was posted to Belzec. He worked as a cook, and trained the Ukrainian guards there before finally being given a new posting to Treblinka as Stangl's deputy.

An SS man poses for the camera with some dogs. Many of the SS men regarded their posting to Treblinka as particularly good, and felt that what they were doing there was right. Although they were taught blind and absolute obedience to all orders from their SS superiors, there were a number of occasions when some felt able to criticize the way the camp was being run. But they never needed to fear reprisal if they criticized an order. Their superiors often allowed officers lower down the chain of command openly to use their initiative and voice their views. They knew that every SS man believed wholeheartedly in the Nazi vision, and for this reason they were relatively free to question the details of how camp management was implemented.

Two officers from Belzec death camp are seen laughing and joking whilst drinking beer. On the left is *SS-Oberscharführer* Heinrich Gley; *SS-Hauptsturmführer* Gottlieb Hering is on the right.

Three women pose for the camera with an SS officer during the winter of late 1942. By this period of the war Operation Reinhard was in full operation.

SS officers stand on the steps of a building sometime during the summer of 1942. By the summer of 1942, both Sobibor and Belzec death camps were running simultaneously, and despite the technical problems of machinery breaking down and the problems with body disposal, the 'Action Reinhard' camps were achieving what they had been intended for, the wholesale mass extermination of the Jews.

SS-Oberscharführer Willy Matzig was a book-keeper/accountant at Treblinka and was one of Stangl's two senior administrative assistants. His office was in Stangl's quarters. He was also part of the squad which received prisoners on the platform when deportations arrived. (H.E.A.R.T)

A portrait photograph of a young SS man. Almost every SS man who worked in the death camps was determined from the onset to conceal as much of the gruesome knowledge of what went on in the camps as possible. In this they were protecting their oaths, but also their own credentials as human beings.

(*Opposite page*) An SS officer at an unidentified camp in the summer of 1942. Many of the new recruits that were picked for Treblinka, and indeed for all the 'Action Reinhard' camps, were individually selected on the basis of their previous experience in the Euthanasia Programme. The main personnel had been administered directly from the officers of T4, all of which boasted an exceptional record. In total only ninety-six SS out of 400 had been chosen to run the three camps. Most of these SS men were now actively playing their part in the extermination of the Jews in Poland, whilst the remaining handful of SS recruited were sent to Treblinka, some of whom had never worked in a concentration camp before.

SS guards stand in formation outside the commandant's house near the Belzec concentration camp.
(*USHMM 87764*)

SS-Oberscharführer Hermann Erich Bauer. He had initially participated in the T4 programme, and then later in Operation Reinhard, serving as a gas chamber operator at Sobibor extermination camp.

Chapter Four

Labour Camp Commandants

Throughout the Nazi empire and the occupied countries, millions regarded by the Germans as 'subhuman' continued to be used either as a labour force, or murdered, preferably by gas. In the many thousands of labour camps that were erected, conditions on site under which the labour force had to work were appalling. Those unfortunate to be incarcerated in these camps had become slaves for the SS, and much of their work was lethal. Many died, and those that survived often suffered permanent injury. Malnourished, badly equipped, lacking protective gear, constantly harassed by the guards, the workers had little chance of surviving the arduous labour.

Under the violent reign of the camp commandant, for example the notorious *SS-Sturmbannfuhrer* Otto Förschner of Mittelbau-Dora concentration camp and the Dachau sub-camp of Kaufering, or *SS-Hauptsturmführer* Amon Goeth of the Kraków-Płaszów concentration camp in Płaszów in German-occupied Poland, many of the inmates were constantly beaten with sticks or truncheons, were shot, or suffered any imaginable form of torture. Those who were ill or too weak to continue working were ordered to be shot in front of the work-detail or dragged away and executed. The other workers were compelled to continue working without pause until the foreman blew his whistle ordering every man to lay down his tools. By the end of the day the majority of the men and women were exhausted. Many were on the point of collapsing, but those who had become too weak to work again the following morning ran the risk of being declared unfit for further work and taken away. Those that had actually died on site from exhaustion or killed for some minor infringement earlier that day were piled up in heaps ready for collection by cart. Early the next morning the foreman would take stock of his workforce. Any person he deemed was no longer able to perform to the satisfaction of the commandant was selected for death.

These commandants knew that the fear of being killed was enough to spur the workers to greater efforts and that they undertook tasks beyond their strength as a result. According to SS reports, injured or ill workers regularly refrained from seeking medical treatment out of terror of being executed. The death and injury rate of the construction gangs was mainly attributed to guards physically abusing their work force.

Camp commandant Amon Goeth was regarded as a loathsome man, even among some of the cruellest guards. Red faced and sweating, he could often be seen screaming obscenities and beating and killing Jews. Prisoners recalled that 'he used to beat the prisoners with a completely expressionless, apathetic look on his face, as if the beatings were part of his daily routine'.

SS-Sturmbannführer Fritz Suhren was another notorious commandant who did not need any encouragement to commit terrible acts of cruelty against his victims. He was commandant of the women's camp at Ravensbrück. His policy upon taking command in 1942 was to exterminate the prisoners through working them as hard as possible and feeding them as little as possible. He enjoyed meting out harsh and brutal punishments for the slightest infractions of camp rules. Anyone he found with smuggled valuables in their possession was either beaten or shot on the spot, in full view of other deportees. He was known among some of his comrades to be an arrogant self-righteous individual with no morals or scruples. Whilst on duty he roamed the camp in an arrogant overbearing manner and would be seen beating, kicking, slapping, and whipping prisoners ruthlessly. His posting as commandant had given him a chance to excel where his life had previously failed him. Now he was able to take great pride in the fact that his mere presence caused the women inmates to tremble with fear. He gleefully followed the policy of controlled and disciplined terror laid down during his guard training. This barbarous man would conduct his cruel beatings with a nonchalant and cavalier attitude. He regularly had the weak shot in full view of the other prisoner workers.

For Suhren, and indeed for many of the commandants, they had manufactured for themselves what they considered to be a tolerable life. Their posting was relatively easy. They had as much food and alcohol to drink as they wanted. Many of the SS camps were very much like small towns. A number of camps had vegetable shops, and you could buy bones to make broth. There was a canteen. Some had cinemas; some had theatres with regular performances. There were sports clubs, and there were dances – all fun and entertainment.

Quite often the commandants held large parties in their villas, where staff could bring members of their families or their girl friends. The relaxed atmosphere was all far removed from the horrors that were taking place elsewhere in the camp. The commandants would encourage such behaviour, almost trying to delude those around them. But they knew, as well as everyone else participating, that it was a big charade. Like so many that endured these terrible circumstances, escapism from reality meant survival.

(*Opposite above*) In Poland in the winter of 1942 a German stands guards on a snow-covered railroad track as a group of Jews are led to a deportation train. (*USHMM 026024*)

(*Opposite below*) A photograph of *SS-Sturmbannführer* Max Pauly talking to other staff officers next to his car. Pauly was the commandant of Stutthof concentration camp from September 1939 to August 1942, and commandant of Neuengamme and its associated subcamps from September 1942 until the end of the war.

(*Above*) Taken in the summer of 1942, this photograph shows *SS-Obersturmbannführer* Arthur Rödl the commandant of Gross-Rosen (in white), in the camp with three members of the SS staff. His adjutant Kuno Schramm is on the right. (*USHMM, courtesy of Martin Mansson 55780*)

(*Opposite page*) Another photograph of Arthur Rödl taken in 1942. (*USHMM Courtesy of Martin Mansson 55808*)

View of the Ravensbrück concentration camp. This photograph is from the *SS-Propaganda-Album des Frauen-KZ-Ravensbrück 1940–1941*.

Camp commandant Karl Ehrlich reviews the child prisoners at his camp. *(USHMM, courtesy of Instytut Pamieci Narodowej 00845)*

An SS guard (possibly Schmiller) supervises work in the Lipa farm labour camp. (*USHMM, courtesy of Oldrich Stransky 51973*)

(*Left*) Two SS officers with a guard dog in the Janowska concentration camp. (*USHMM, courtesy of Herman Lewinter 69984*)

(*Right*) An SS man poses for the camera in the summer of 1941. Life for these men was relatively easy. Whatever thoughts some of the less susceptible SS men had on how the concentration camps were run were suppressed. They were able to bury their emotions and enjoy the camaraderie that came with being a loyal member of the SS.

An SS man relaxes while off duty. The more ambitious concentration camp guard could learn from his commandant. If they were to progress through the ranks, they needed to strengthen their belief that all the prisoners detained inside the system were inferior, and implacable enemies of the state.

A group of SS officers, a woman and a dog stand on the grounds of the Gross-Rosen concentration camp. *SS-Obersturmführer* Anton Thumann is pictured third from the right. Thumann was a *Schutzhaftlagerführer* (Protective Custody Camp Leader) in various concentration camps. *(USHMM, courtesy of Martin Mansson 36226)*

(*Above*) Three members of the SS staff in Gross-Rosen pose holding six piglets. The adjutant to the commandant, Kuno Schramm, is standing on the left. (*USHMM, courtesy of Martin Mansson 55779*)

(*Opposite page*) *SS-Reichsführer* Heinrich Himmler (right) shakes the hand of camp commandant *SS-Hauptsturmführer* Friedrich Warzok during an official tour of a Jewish labour camp along the main supply route in Galicia. (*USHMM 82795*)

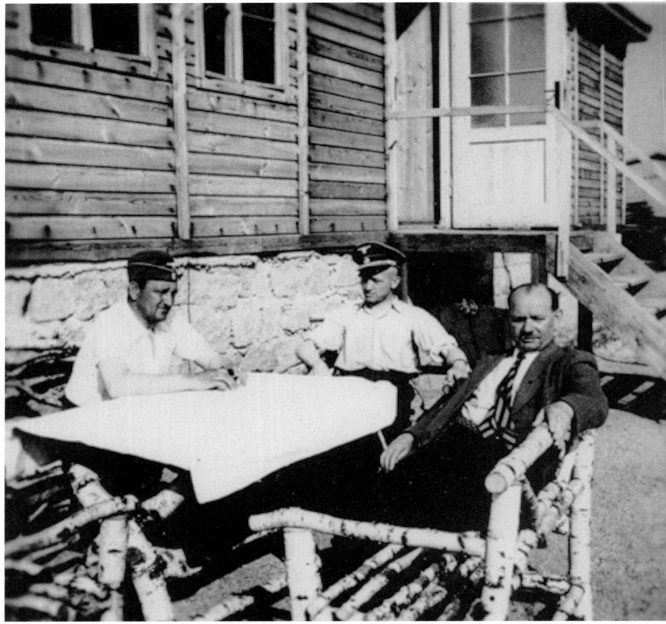

(*Above*) SS officers and an unidentified man sit at a picnic table outside a building at the Gross-Rosen concentration camp. Pictured on the left is the commandant, Arthur Rödl. His adjutant, Kuno Schramm is in the centre. (*USHMM, courtesy of Martin Mansson 36225*)

(*Opposite above*) View of a wooden building and surrounding garden (probably the home of an SS officer) in the Hinzert concentration camp (sub-camp of Buchenwald). (*USHMM, courtesy of Robert A. Schmuhl 23664*)

(*Opposite below*) An SS officer, Commandant Hermann Pister, relaxes on the porch of a building with a woman and another man. (*USHMM, courtesy of Robert A. Schmuhl 23656*)

Four SS officers, including Commandant Hermann Pister, have a conversation in the grounds of the Hinzert concentration camp. (*USHMM, courtesy of Robert A. Schmuhl 23666*)

Camp guards beat a prisoner at the Cieszanow labour camp. (*USHMM, courtesy of Jerzy Tomaszewski 05063*)

Two photographs showing the notorious *SS-Hauptsturmführer* Amon Goeth. He was commandant of the Krakow-Plaszow concentration camp in Plaszow in German-occupied Poland. Goeth was a loathsome commandant, and was responsible for many random and brutal killings. (*M. Kaludow*)

Prisoners at forced labour in the Neuengamme concentration camp. (*USHMM, courtesy of KZ-Gedenkstatte Neuengamme 06031*)

SS men sometime in 1943. By this period of the war the concentration camp system was in full operation with many millions of people regarded by the Nazi regime as hostile being shipped to labour camps, concentration camps or murdered in the death camps.

Belsen locals enjoy a beer with an SS commanding officer. Behind this façade the SS men were hiding terrible truths about their posting, and avoided ever uttering a word about them outside the camp. Local inhabitants were not aware of the barbaric measures taken against the inmates in the camp.

SS-Hauptsturmführer commandant Josef Kramer. In December 1944, Kramer was transferred from Birkenau to Bergen Belsen where he was promoted to commandant. Kramer's regime was so barbaric that he became known as the 'Beast of Belsen'. Even as the Reich became squeezed by the advance of both Soviet and Allied troops, and the administration of the camp broke down, Kramer continued his reign of terror on the inmates.

(*Above*) Kramer and Irma Grese are seen here together just before their trial. Grese was a young female guard whose name was synonymous with brutality to inmates. Hardened from working at Auschwitz she came to Belsen and continued to uphold her barbaric reputation. Strutting around the camp with her black boots, whip, and smart SS uniform, she daily looked for victims she could torture or kill. Irma's sadistic lust for torture and murder eventually saw her being sent to the gallows in December 1945 for crimes against humanity. Kramer authorized Grese to have her permanent assignment at Belsen and was reputed to be one of her many lovers. (*BU-9745, Imperial War Museum*)

(*Opposite page*) Two photographs showing a shackled Josef Kramer, commandant of Belsen, who has been arrested by British troops and is being escorted away under armed guard. Prior to the liberation of Belsen, the camp had descended into chaos, and Kramer could no longer cope with the amount of new arrivals. He became particularly scathing towards his subordinates and forced them to commit bestial acts. Now guards who had shown some degree of restraint towards the deportees would whip and beat woman and children. Some murdered them with their own hands and shot dead anyone who would not respond quickly enough to an order. (*BU-3822, BU37-49, Imperial War Museum*)

Three photographs of Commandant Hermann Pister. One photograph shows Pister overseeing a column of prisoners in Buchenwald sub-camp. The other two show him leaving what appears to be an administration building.

(*USHMM, courtesy of Robert A. Schmuhl*)

(*Above*) *SS-Oberführer* Hans Loritz, commandant of Sachsenhausen (centre), visits the Gross-Rosen concentration camp. Also pictured are Arthur Rödl (left), Friedrich Entress (second from the left), Hans Loritz, Michl, Hubert Lauer (Administrator head of Sachsenhausen) (second from right), and Anton Thumann (far right). (*USHMM, courtesy of Martin Mansson A. Haag 55778*)

(*Opposite above*) View of the construction of the Mauthausen-Gusen I concentration camp. Mauthausen-Gusen grew to become a large group of concentration camps in Upper Austria (National Archives)

(*Opposite below*) Rudolf Höss, commandant of Auschwitz from its inception in 1940 until late 1943. On 25 May 1946, Höss left Nuremberg with his wrists manacled by heavy-duty handcuffs. He was hastily driven to the airport with Dr von Burgsdorff and Josef Bühler where an American aircraft flew them to Warsaw via Berlin. When they arrived at the airport in Warsaw under armed guard they were greeted by the Press. Under the spotlight of the Press and shouts and screams of abuse from the many onlookers, they were officially handed over to the Polish authorities and escorted by car to a Warsaw prison. A year later on 16 April 1947, Höss was finally led from the prison and escorted by heavy guard to Auschwitz, to the same building where he had presided over the fate of thousands of people and hanged. Rudolf Höss had finally received retribution for all those that perished in his hands. He never made any public statement about what he had done, nor did he utter a word about the glory of the Nazi ideology that he had died for. (*USHMM*)

A group of SS officers stand on the steps of a building at the Gross-Rosen concentration camp. Standing on the far left is the adjutant, Kuno Schramm. Michl is standing behind him on the top left. The commandant Arthur Rödl is on the top right. Beneath him is Anton Thumann (bottom right). (*USHMM, courtesy of Martin Mansson 36224*)

SS officers bid farewell to SS platoon squad commander Schramm at Gross-Rosen. Anton Thumann is pictured fifth from left. Artur Rödl is in the front centre. Kuno Schramm is in the first row, far right. Standing third from the left is probably Dr Friedrich Entress. (*USHMM, courtesy of Martin Mansson A. Haag 55777*)

(*Above*) Franz Ziereis poses in front of the commandant's headquarters on the wall overlooking the garage courtyard (*Garagenhofmauer*) in Mauthausen. (*USHMM, courtesy of Andras Tsagatakis 76514*)

(*Opposite page*) *SS-Hauptsturmführer* Georg Bachmaier, deputy to Commandant Franz Ziereis in Mauthausen, inspects a group of prisoners at forced labour constructing the 'Russian camp'. (*USHMM, courtesy of Archiv der KZ-Gedenkstaette Mauthausen 5062*)

(*Below*) *Unterscharführer* Lubasik, commandant of the Siemens Schuckert works at Bobrek, leans out of an open window at a barracks. (*Henry Schwarzbaum 95287*)

(*Above*) Group portrait of SS officers at the Gross-Rosen concentration camp. The commandant Arthur Rödl is in the centre. Second from the left is probably Dr Friedrich Entress. *SS-Ostuf* Anton Thumann is in the first row, right. (*USHMM, courtesy of Martin Mansson 36221*)

(*Opposite above*) SS guard Schmiller walks past the barn of the Lipa farm labour camp where Jewish workers are pitching hay. Lipa concentration camp or *Umschulungslager Linden bei Deutsch-Brod* was established in Havlickuv Brod in 1940 by the *Zentralstelle für Jüdische Auswanderung* (Central Office for Jewish Emigration), an authority co-ordinating all activities associated with Jews after the Protectorate of Bohemia and Moravia had been constituted in March 1939. (*USHMM, courtesy of Oldrich Stransky 51970*)

(*Opposite below*) SS guard Schmiller stands on a dirt road in the Lipa farm labour camp with his dog. (*USHMM, courtesy of Oldrich Stransky 51971*)

(*Above*) Close-up portrait of three SS officers in Gross-Rosen. Pictured on the far right is the adjutant Kuno Schramm. (*USHMM, courtesy of Martin Mansson 55801*)

(*Opposite above*) Jewish deportees under German guard march through the streets of Kamenets-Podolsk to an execution site outside the city. (*USHMM, courtesy of Ivan Sved 28215*)

(*Opposite below*) Murdered SS men lie next to a wall at Dachau. After liberation many SS men were killed on the spot by both their liberators and their former prisoners. (*USHMM*)

(*Above*) Group portrait of four SS officers at the Gross-Rosen concentration camp. Arthur Rödl is standing on the far left. Next to him is Anton Thumann. An inscription on the back identifies one of the other two men as *SS-Obersturmführer* Drosenhofer. (*USHMM, courtesy of Martin Mansson 55763*)

(*Opposite above*) SS officers sit in a classroom in the Hinzert concentration camp (a sub-camp of Buchenwald). (*USHMM, courtesy of Robert A. Schmuhl 23667*)

(*Opposite below*) A group of SS officers tour the Hinzert concentration camp. (*USHMM, courtesy of Robert A. Schmuhl 34561*)

(*Above*) *SS-Obergruppenführer* Ernst Schmauser visits the Gross-Rosen concentration camp's quarry with other SS officers. Commandant Arthur Rödl is standing next to Schmauser in the centre. (*USHMM, courtesy of Martin Mansson 36223*)

(*Opposite above*) Heinrich Himmler and a group of SS officers inspecting the Janowska concentration camp. (*USHMM 69979*)

(*Opposite below*) *SS-Obergruppenführer* Ernst Schmauser inspects the Gross-Rosen concentration camp in the company of other SS officers. Schmauser is pictured third from the left. Arthur Rödl is next to him in the centre. Rödl's adjutant, Kuno Schramm is the officer on the far right. (*USHMM, courtesy of Martin Mansson 36222*)

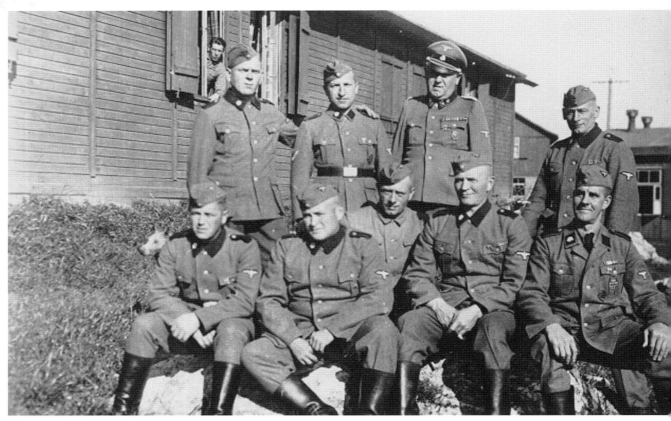

A group of SS guards with their commandant posing for the camera. (*USHMM, courtesy of Robert A. Schmuhl 34559*)

Appendix I

Concentration Camp Commandants 1933–1945

Richard Baer (9 September 1911 – 17 June 1963)
German Nazi official with the rank of *SS-Sturmbannführer* and commander of the Auschwitz I concentration camp from May 1944 to February 1945.

Hermann Baranowski (11 June 1884 in Schwerin – 5 February 1940 in Aue)
A German politician and military figure. Commandant of two German concentration camps of the SS Death's Head unit. He was the commandant of Dachau concentration camp in 1938. He served as the *SS-Oberführer* of Sachsenhausen concentration camp from February 1938 to September 1939.

Hans Bothmann (11 November 1911 – 4 April 1946)
Holding the rank of *SS-Hauptsturmführer* he was the last commandant of the Chełmno extermination camp from 1942 on (SS card number 117630); he was leader of the *SS Special Detachment Bothmann* conducting the extermination of Jews from the Łódź Ghetto and other places. He committed suicide in British custody in April 1946 while in Heide.

Alois Brunner (born 8 April 1912)
An Austrian SS officer and became Adolf Eichmann's assistant. Eichmann referred to Brunner as his best man. Brunner is held responsible for sending at least 140,000 European Jews to the gas chambers. He was commander of the Drancy internment camp outside Paris from June 1943 to August 1944, from which nearly 24,000 people were deported. He was condemned to death *in absentia* in France in 1954 for crimes against humanity.

Karl Chmielewski (born 16 July 1903 in Frankfurt am Main;
died 1 December 1991 in Bernau am Chiemsee)
A German SS officer and concentration camp commandant. Such was his cruelty that he was dubbed *Teufel von Gusen* or the Devil of Gusen.

Heinrich Deubel (19 February 1890 – 2 October 1962)
A German soldier, civil servant and officer in the SS who served as commandant of Dachau concentration camp.

Irmfried Eberl (8 September 1910 – 16 February 1948)
An Austrian Nazi, he held the rank of *SS-Obersturmführer*. He assisted in the creation of the Treblinka extermination camp and was its first commandant, where he worked from 11 July 1942 until his dismissal on 26 August 1942. As a psychiatrist, Eberl was the only physician to command an extermination camp. In January 1948 he was arrested. Before his trial could begin, he hanged himself.

Theodor Eicke (17 October 1892 – 26 February 1943)
An *SS-Obergruppenführer*, commander of the SS-Division (mot) *Totenkopf* of the *Waffen-SS* and one of the key figures in the establishment of concentration camps.

Walter Eisfeld (born 11 July 1905 in Halle, Saxony-Anhalt; died 3 April 1940 in Dachau)
An SS officer and Nazi concentration camp commandant.

Hermann Florstedt (18 February 1895 – 15 April 1945)
Became the third Commandant of Majdanek concentration camp in October 1942. He was executed by the SS in 1945.

Otto Förschner (4 November 1902 – 28 May 1946)
German *SS-Sturmbannfuhrer* and Nazi concentration camp officer. Commandant of the Mittelbau-Dora concentration camp and the Dachau sub-camp of Kaufering.

Kurt Franz (17 January 1914 – 4 July 1998)
An SS officer and one of the commanders of the Treblinka extermination camp.

Karl Fritzsch (Born 10 July 1903; went missing 2 May 1945)
Held the rank of *SS-Hauptsturmführer* and was a concentration camp officer at Auschwitz and deputy. He first suggested and experimented with using Zyklon-B gas for the purpose of mass murder.

Wilhelm Gideon (15 November 1898 in Oldenburg, died after 1975)
An SS officer and was appointed commandant of Gross-Rosen concentration camp on 16 September 1942 in succession to Arthur Rödl. He held the post until 10 October 1943 when Johannes Hassebroek succeeded him.

Amon Goeth (11 December 1908 – 13 September 1946)
An Austrian *SS-Hauptsturmführer* and the commandant of the Kraków-Płaszów concentration camp in Płaszów in German-occupied Poland.

Fritz Hartjenstein (3 July 1905 – 20 October 1954)
An *SS-Obersturmbannführer*, *Totenkopfverbände*. He worked at various concentration camps such as Auschwitz and Sachsenhausen.

Johannes Hassebroek (11 July 1910 in Halle, Saxony-Anhalt – 17 April 1977 in Westerstede)
An officer and commandant of Gross-Rosen concentration camp in succession to Wilhelm Gideon in October 1943.

Hans Helwig (25 September 1881 in Hemsbach – 24 August 1952 also in Hemsbach)
A Nazi politician, SS general and concentration camp commandant. Initially he became commandant of the women's camp at Lichtenburg. In July 1937 he succeeded Karl Otto Koch as commandant of Sachsenhausen concentration camp.

Gottlieb Hering (2 June 1887 – 9 October 1945)
An *SS-Hauptsturmführer* who served in Action T4 and later as the second and last commandant of Bełżec extermination camp during Operation Reinhard.

Paul-Werner Hoppe (28 February 1910 – 15 July 1974)
An *SS-Sturmbannführer* and was the commandant of Stutthof concentration camp from September 1942 until April 1945.

Rudolf Höss (25 November 1901 – 16 April 1947)
An *SS-Obersturmbannführer*, and from 4 May 1940 to November 1943 was the commandant of Auschwitz concentration camp.

Anton Kaindl (14 July 1902, Munich – 1948 in Vorkuta)
An *SS-Standartenführer* and commandant of the Sachsenhausen concentration camp from 1942-1945.

Karl-Otto Koch (2 August 1897 – 5 April 1945)
Holding the rank of *SS-Standartenführer* he was the first commandant of the concentration camps at Buchenwald and Sachsenhausen. From September 1941 until August 1942 Koch served as the first commandant of the Majdanek concentration camp in occupied Poland.

Max Koegel (16 October 1895 – 27 June 1946)
An SS officer who served as a commander at Lichtenburg, Ravensbrück, Majdanek and Flossenbürg concentration camps.

Josef Kramer (10 November 1906 – 13 December 1945)
The commandant of the Bergen-Belsen concentration camp, dubbed '*The Beast of Belsen*' by camp inmates.

Herbert Lange (29 September 1909 – 20 April 1945)
A *Sturmbannführer* in the SS and the commandant of Chełmno extermination camp until April 1942; he was leader of the *SS Special Detachment Lange* conducting the extermination of Jews from the Łódź Ghetto.

Arthur Liebehenschel (25 November 1901 – 28 January 1948)
A commandant at the Auschwitz and Majdanek death camps.

Michael Lippert (24 April 1897 – 1 September 1969)
He held the position of *SS-Standartenführer*, and commanded several concentration camps, including Sachsenhausen, before becoming a commander of the *SS-Freiwilligen Legion Flandern* and the *10 SS-Panzer-Division, Frundsberg*.

Hans Loritz (12 December 1895 – 31 January 1946)
Commandant at camp Papenburg and Esterwegen, he was then transferred to commandant of Dachau until 1939. In 1940 he was posted to Sachsenhausen, and in 1942 was removed and sent to oversee a camp in Norway.

Max Pauly
SS-Standartenführer, commandant of Stutthof concentration camp from September 1939 to August 1942 and commandant of Neuengamme concentration camp and the associated sub-camps from September 1942 until the end of the war in 1945.

Hermann Pister
SS-Oberführer and commandant of Buchenwald concentration camp from 21 January 1942 until April 1945.

Kurt Pompe
Commandant in a number of forced labour camps for Jews in Silesia until the end of the war, part of a huge network of over 160 camps run by an SS organization known as *Dienststelle Schmelt*.

Franz Reichleitner
SS-Hauptsturmführer serving in Operation Reinhard. He served as the second and last commandant of Sobibor death camp from 1 September 1942 until the camp's closure on about 17 October 1943. He was directly responsible for the wholesale murder of the Jews at Sobibor.

Arthur Rödl
SS-Standartenführer, *Waffen-SS*, deputy-commandant at Buchenwald, eventually given a command of the Gross-Rosen concentration camp.

Heinrich Schwarz
SS-Hauptsturmführer and concentration camp officer, stationed at Mauthausen and Sachsenhausen concentration camps during 1940–1941. He also served as commandant of Auschwitz III-Monowitz and Natzweiler-Struthof in Alsace-Lorraine.

Franz Stangl
SS-Hauptsturmführer, an Austrian, graduate of Hartheim 'euthanasia' centre. He later became commandant of the Sobibor and Treblinka extermination camps during Operation Reinhard.

Karl Streibel

SS-Hauptsturmführer, the second and last commander of the Trawniki concentration camp, one of the sub-camps of the KL Lublin system of concentration camps in occupied Poland.

Fritz Suhren

SS-Sturmbannführer, was initially stationed at Sachsenhausen concentration camp in 1941. Later he became commandant of the women's camp at Ravensbrück.

Richard Thomalla

SS-Hauptsturmführer, headed construction of the Reinhard camps, Belzec, Sobibor and Treblinka.

Lotte Toberentz

Commander of the Uckermark concentration camp for girls. From December 1944 to April 1945, *Lagerführerin* (camp leader) of the Ravensbrück concentration camp.

Hilmar Wäckerle

Chosen by Himmler to be commandant of the newly-established Dachau concentration camp in 1933, he left his post a few months later. During the war he was a member of the *Waffen-SS* and served with the 5th SS Panzer Division Wiking.

Martin Gottfried Weiss

SS-Obersturmbannführer, served as the commandant of Neuengamme concentration camp from April 1940 until September 1942, and was the Majdanek death camp's fourth commandant from November 1943 until May 1944. His last posting was commandant of Dachau where he was in 1945 at the time of his arrest.

Christian Wirth

SS-Sturmbannführer, was a German policeman and SS officer who was one of the leading architects of the program to exterminate the Jewish population of Poland, known as Operation Reinhard. Wirth served as Inspector of all Operation Reinhard camps. He was commandant of Chełmno and Bełżec extermination camps during most of their operation.

Franz Ziereis

SS-Standartenführer, became commandant of Mauthausen on 9 February 1939.

Egon Zill

He was commandant of Natzweiler-Struthof before taking charge at Flossenbürg. He was later transferred to the Eastern Front in 1943.

Appendix II

Glossary and Abbreviations

Einsatzgruppen – Mobile killing units of the SS, Sipo-SD.

Gau – One of forty-two Nazi Party administrative districts into which Nazi Germany was divided.

Gauleiter – Nazi Party boss in a Gau.

General Government – Occupied part of eastern Poland not annexed to Germany.

Gestapo – Geheime Staatspolizei: state secret police.

Reichsführer-SS – Reich Chief of the SS and German Police.

RSHA – *Reichssicherheitshauptamt*: Reich Main Security Office, formed in late 1939, uniting Gestapo, criminal police, SIPO and SD.

SD – Sicherheitsdienst: security service of the Nazi Party.

Sonderkommando – Special unit of SS.

SS – Schutzstaffel: Guard Detachment created in 1925 as elite Nazi Party bodyguard that evolved as a security and intelligence service with a military arm.

Totenkopf – *Totenkopfverbande*: Death's Head, unit of SS deployed to guard concentration camps.

Waffen-SS – Weapon SS: Military arm of the SS from 1939 onwards.

Wehrmacht – German armed forces.

WVHA – *Wirtschaffts und Verwaltungshauptamt*: SS Economic and Administrative Head Office, responsible for SS economic enterprises and concentration camps from 1942 under the command of Oswald Pohl.

Rank Equivalents

German Army	Waffen-SS	British Army
Gemeiner, Landser	Schütze	Private
	Oberschütze	
Grenadier	Sturmmann	Lance Corporal
Obergrenadier		
Gefreiter	Rottenführer	Corporal
Obergefreiter	Unterscharführer	
Stabsgefreiter		
Unteroffizier	Scharführer	Sergeant
Unterfeldwebel	Oberscharführer	Colour Sergeant
Feldwebel		
Oberfeldwebel	Hauptscharführer	Sergeant Major
Stabsfeldwebel	Hauptbereitschaftsleiter	
	Sturmscharführer	Warrant Officer
Leutnant	Untersturmführer	Second Lieutenant
Oberleutnant	Obersturmführer	First Lieutenant
Hauptmann	Hauptsturmführer	Captain
Major	Sturmbannführer	Major
Oberstleutnant	Obersturmbannführer	Lieutenant Colonel
Oberst	Standartenführer	Colonel
	Oberführer	Brigadier General
Generalmajor	Brigadeführer	Major General
Generalleutnant	Gruppenführer	Lieutenant General
General	Obergruppenführer	General
Generaloberst	Oberstgruppenführer	
Generalfeldmarschall	Reichsführer-SS	